GW01117305

QUICK & EASY COOKING

FOR BEGINNERS

Jamie Romier

Table of Contents

APPETIZING BITES FOR DOURING THE DAY 7

Asparagus Wrapped In Crisp Prosciutto 8

Avocado And Sun Dried Tomato Spring Rolls 10

Avocado And Tuna Tapas 13

Baba Ghanoush 15

Crispy Tuna Croquettes 17

Crostini Alla Fiorentina 20

Crostini With Mozzarella And Tomato 23

Daddy Mack's Oysters 25

Date Goat Cheese Basil Bites 27

Deep Fried Sous Vide Egg Yolks 29

Drenched Fig Boats 31

Frozen Grapes 33

Ahi Poke Basic 35

Apricot Pecan Camembert 37

Arancini (Italian Rice Balls) 39

Asian Roll Lettuce Wrap 42

Asparagus Rolantina 45

Baba Ghanuj 46

Bacon Wrapped Dates Stuffed With Blue Cheese 49

Baked Goat Cheese Caprese Salad 51

Baked Pork Spring Rolls... 53

Baked Stuffed Brie With Cranberries Walnuts............ 55

Barney's King Salmon Gravlax....................................... 58

Beef Samosas 60

Oyster Motoyaki 63

Blue Cheese And Pear Tartlets....................................... 66

Boranie Bademjan (Persian Eggplant Yogurt Dip) 68

Brie And Mushroom Phyllo Puffs 70

Broiled Mochi With Nori Seaweed 73

Bruschetta With Roasted Sweet Red Peppers.............. 75

Buckwheat Grissini With Real Butter (Gluten Free) ... 77

Buddhist Monk Dumplings.. 79

Burrata Bruschetta With Figs 82

Cantonese Style Pork And Shrimp Dumplings 84

Caponata Sauce... 86

- Chef John's Asparagus Tart 89
- Pate De Campagne 91
- Chevre With Urfa And Crushed Nibs 95
- Chicken Liver Pate 97
- Chicken, Artichoke, And Spinach Stuffed Portobellos 99
- Chinese Tea Leaf Eggs 102
- Chocolate Sea Salt Crostini 104
- Chourico Breakfast Salsa 106
- Cold Roasted Moroccan Spiced Salmon 108
- Crab Stuffed Mushrooms 111
- Crab And Lobster Stuffed Mushrooms 113
- Creamy Garlic Escargot 115
- THANK YOU 119

APPETIZING BITES FOR DOURING THE DAY

Asparagus Wrapped In Crisp Prosciutto

Serving: 16

Ingredients

- 1 tablespoon olive oil
- 16 spears fresh asparagus, trimmed
- 16 slices prosciutto

Direction

- Set an oven to preheat to 220°C (450°F). Use aluminum foil to line a baking sheet and coat it using olive oil.
- Wrap each asparagus spear with 1 slice of prosciutto, beginning at the bottom and spiral it up to the tip. Put the wrapped spares on the prepped baking sheet.
- Let it bake in the preheated oven for 5 minutes. Take it out and shake the pan back and forth to roll over the spears. Put it back into the oven for an additional of 5 minutes or until the prosciutto becomes crisp and the asparagus becomes tender. Serve it right away.

Nutrition Information

- Calories: 64 calories;
- Total Fat: 5.4
- Sodium: 279
- Total Carbohydrate: 0.6
- Cholesterol: 13
- Protein: 3.1

Avocado And Sun Dried Tomato Spring Rolls

Serving: 8

Ingredients

- onion 1 teaspoon lemon juice
- 8 spring roll wrappers
- 1/4 cup diced green onion
- 2 tablespoons finely chopped shiitake mushrooms
- 1/3 cup sun-dried tomatoes, chopped
- salt and pepper to taste
- 2 ounces boneless chicken breast halves, cooked and diced
- 1 quart oil for frying
- 2 tablespoons vegetable oil
- 1/3 cup shredded cabbage
- 1/4 cup shredded carrots
- 1/4 cup shredded cucumber

- 2 tablespoons diced 1 ounce cooked crabmeat, diced
- 1 teaspoon Chinese five-spice powder
- 1 avocado - peeled, pitted and diced

Direction

- In a wok, heat one-quart oil on moderately-high heat.
- In medium-size saucepan, heat 2 tablespoons of oil on moderate heat. Mix in pepper, salt, sun-dried tomatoes, shiitake mushrooms, green onion, onion, cucumber, carrots and cabbage. Cook and mix slowly for 10 minutes, till every vegetable soften.
- Mix crabmeat, Chinese five-spice powder and chicken in mixture of cabbage. Drizzle lemon juice on avocado, then mix into mixture. Take off from heat.
- Put chicken mixture and about a teaspoon cabbage in spring roll wrappers' middle. Fold the wrappers, and moisten your fingers then enclose edges.

- Put spring rolls down in warm quart of oil carefully. Deep fry till golden brown, for about 3 minutes. Transfer onto paper towels to drain. Halve and serve.

Nutrition Information

- Calories: 208 calories;
- Protein: 4
- Total Fat: 18.8
- Sodium: 71
- Total Carbohydrate: 7.3
- Cholesterol: 8

Avocado And Tuna Tapas

Serving: 4

Ingredients

- 1 dash balsamic vinegar
- black pepper to taste
- 1 pinch garlic salt, or to taste
- 1 (12 ounce) can solid white tuna packed in water, drained
- 1 tablespoon mayonnaise
- 3 green onions, thinly sliced, plus additional for garnish
- 1/2 red bell pepper, chopped
- 2 ripe avocados, halved and pitted

Direction

- In a bowl, mix balsamic vinegar, red pepper, green onion, mayonnaise and tuna.
- Add garlic salt and pepper to season.
- Fill the avocado halves with the tuna mixture. Decorate with reserved green onions and a sprinkle of black pepper then serve.

Nutrition Information

- Calories: 294 calories;
- Sodium: 154
- Total Carbohydrate: 11
- Cholesterol: 27
- Protein: 23.9
- Total Fat: 18.2

Baba Ghanoush

Serving: 12

Ingredients

- 1 eggplant
- 1/4 cup lemon juice
- 1/4 cup tahini
- 2 tablespoons sesame seeds
- 2 cloves garlic, minced
- salt and pepper to taste
- 1 1/2 tablespoons olive oil

Direction

- Set an oven to 200°C (400°F) and start preheating. Oil a baking sheet lightly.
- On the greased baking sheet, arrange eggplant; use a fork create holes in the skin. Roast and turn from time to time until it becomes soft, 30-40 minutes. Take it out from the oven and put into a large bowl of cold water. Take out from the water and peel off the skin.

- In an electric blender, puree garlic, sesame seeds, tahini, lemon juice, and eggplant. Use pepper and salt to season. Place the eggplant mixture into a medium-size mixing bowl and gradually stir in olive oil. Before serving, put in the fridge for 3 hours. .

Nutrition Information

- Calories: 66 calories;
- Total Fat: 5.2
- Sodium: 7
- Total Carbohydrate: 4.6
- Cholesterol: 0
- Protein: 1.6

Crispy Tuna Croquettes

Serving: 8

Ingredients

- Garlic Aioli:
- 1 egg yolk, at room temperature
- 3 large cloves garlic, minced
- 1 tablespoon lemon juice
- 5 tablespoons extra-virgin olive oil
- 5 tablespoons canola oil
- salt and ground black pepper to taste
- 1 pinch Spanish paprika
- Croquettes:
- 1/4 cup butter
- 1/4 cup all-purpose flour
- 3/4 cup milk
- 1 (5 ounce) can solid white albacore tuna in water (such as Bumble Bee®)
- 1 tablespoon chopped fresh flat-leaf parsley
- 1 tablespoon chopped fresh chives
- 1 tablespoon chopped fresh dill
- 1/2 teaspoon lemon juice

- 1/2 teaspoon lemon zest
- 1 dash ground nutmeg
- salt and ground black pepper to taste
- 2 eggs
- 2 cups panko bread crumbs
- vegetable oil for frying

Direction

- In a bowl, beat 1 tablespoon lemon juice, garlic, and egg yolk until well combined. Slowly drizzle in a tablespoon canola and olive oil; whisk constantly until well combined. Pour in the leftover canola and olive oil while continuously whisking until the mixture is smooth and thick. Sprinkle paprika, pepper, and salt to season. Refrigerate the aioli.
- On medium-low heat, melt butter in a pan. Mix in flour for a minute to form a paste; turn to low heat. Gradually whisk in milk for 2-3 minutes until the sauce is thick. Mix in nutmeg, tuna, lemon zest, parsley, half teaspoon lemon juice, chives, and dill. Cook and stir for 3 minutes until the mixture resembles the thickness of mashed potatoes. Sprinkle pepper and salt to season.
- In a baking dish, evenly spread the tuna mixture; use a plastic wrap to cover. Refrigerate for 2-3 hours or overnight.

- Beat two eggs in a bowl.
- Place the panko breadcrumbs in a shallow container.
- Split the chilled tuna mixture into eight equal parts. Moisten your hand and form the mixture into cylinders or patties. Submerge patties in egg wash and dredge in bread crumbs to cover; put patties on a plate. Refrigerate for an hour until the patties are firm.
- In a deep fryer or a big pot, heat vegetable oil to 175°C or 350°F.
- Fry croquettes for 5-8 minutes until golden; work in batches. Use a slotted spoon to transfer the croquettes on paper towels to drain. Serve croquettes with aioli.

Nutrition Information

- Calories: 370 calories;
- Sodium: 248
- Total Carbohydrate: 24
- Cholesterol: 94
- Protein: 10.2
- Total Fat: 29.1

Crostini Alla Fiorentina

Serving: 4

Ingredients

- 3 tablespoons olive oil
- 1 teaspoon chopped onion
- 1 teaspoon celery, chopped
- 1 chopped carrot
- 2 cloves garlic, pressed
- 4 ounces chicken livers, rinsed and sliced into strips
- 4 ounces lamb or pork livers, rinsed and cut into strips
- 1/2 cup red wine
- 1 tablespoon tomato puree
- 2 tablespoons chopped fresh parsley
- 3 anchovy fillets, chopped
- 2 tablespoons chicken stock or water
- salt and pepper to taste
- 1 tablespoon butter, or as needed
- 1 tablespoon capers

Direction

- Place a skillet on the stove and turn on to low heat then put the oil. Add in the garlic, carrot, celery and onion; stir and cook for about 5 minutes until onions are softened.
- Pat dry the lamb and chicken liver, then add in to the skillet. Cook on low heat until every sides turned to brown in color. Stir in the red wine over the liver, and let it evaporate in a minute. Mix in the pepper, salt, chicken stock, anchovies, half of parsley, and tomato puree. Cover with a lid and gently boil for 20 minutes and mix in the left parsley, capers and butter.
- Puree the liver mixture using a hand- held blender. Send it to a food processor if you don't have a hand-held blender and mix blend well until becomes smooth. Put it back to the skillet, and mix in the left parsley, capers and butter.

Nutrition Information

- Calories: 224 calories;
- Total Fat: 16.1
- Sodium: 273
- Total Carbohydrate: 2.5
- Cholesterol: 212
- Protein: 11.7

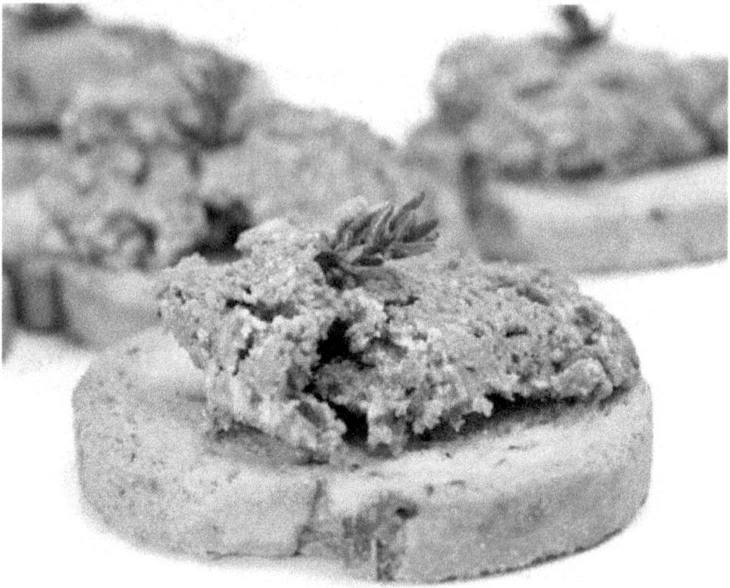

Crostini With Mozzarella And Tomato

Serving: 8

Ingredients

- 1 French baguette, cut into diagonal 1/2 inch slices
- 3 tablespoons extra virgin olive oil
- 4 cloves garlic, halved
- 6 plum tomatoes, seeded and chopped
- 1 bunch fresh basil, julienned
- 1 pound fresh mozzarella cheese, sliced

Direction

- Start preheating the oven's broiler. Use olive oil to brush the bread slices and put on a cookie sheet. Put in the preheated oven and toast under the broiler for about 3 minutes. Watch closely. Rub a garlic clove on each crostini for flavor.

- In a medium-sized bowl, put tomatoes, and use olive oil to sprinkle. Use pepper and salt to season.
- Put the crostini on a serving tray. Put a mozzarella cheese slice on top of each crostini, use 1 spoonful of tomatoes to cover, and use fresh basil to garnish.

Nutrition Information

- Calories: 385 calories;
- Sodium: 453
- Total Carbohydrate: 35.9
- Cholesterol: 45
- Protein: 17.6
- Total Fat: 18.4

Daddy Mack's Oysters

Serving: 6

Ingredients

- 1 cup butter, softened
- 2 tablespoons chopped fresh cilantro
- 3 tablespoons minced garlic
- 2 tablespoons minced shallot
- 2 tablespoons lime juice
- 3 tablespoons chile-garlic sauce (such as Sriracha®)
- 12 fresh oysters in shells
- 2 tablespoons lime juice

Direction

- Mix Sriracha sauce, 2 tbsp. lime juice, shallot, garlic, cilantro and butter in a medium bowl. Spoon on waxed paper. Roll to a log. Put into freeze until its set.
- Preheat grill to high heat.

- Put whole oysters until nearly done for 3-5 minutes on the hot grill. Remove top shell from oysters, don't spill liqueur.
- Put back on grill. Slice butter log to 1/4-inch slices and put on top pf each oyster.
- Grill until butter melts. Serve on a rock salt bed for presentation.

Nutrition Information

- Calories: 304 calories;
- Cholesterol: 89
- Protein: 3.7
- Total Fat: 31
- Sodium: 550
- Total Carbohydrate: 4.2

Date Goat Cheese Basil Bites

Serving: 20

Ingredients

- 1 (8 ounce) package goat cheese, slightly softened
- 1 1/2 tablespoons honey
- 3 tablespoons chopped fresh basil
- 1 pound pitted dates
- 1/3 pound thinly sliced prosciutto
- toothpicks

Direction

- In a bowl, mix basil, honey, and goat cheese until creamy and smooth; chill in 20 minutes.
- Preheat oven or toaster oven at 400°F (200°C).
- Use a tiny spoon to fill dates with goat cheese filling.

- Entirely cover each date with enough prosciutto and secure with a toothpick. Line them on a baking sheet.
- Roast in the preheated toaster oven in about 10 minutes, until prosciutto turns caramelized and crisp.
- Turn over each date, go on baking for 5 minutes more until crisp on top.

Nutrition Information

- Calories: 138 calories;
- Total Fat: 5.9
- Sodium: 205
- Total Carbohydrate: 18.6
- Cholesterol: 16
- Protein: 4.5

Deep Fried Sous Vide Egg Yolks

Serving: 6

Ingredients

- 7 eggs, divided
- 1/3 cup all-purpose flour
- 1 teaspoon sea salt
- 1/2 teaspoon baking powder
- 1/2 cup fine bread crumbs
- canola oil for frying
- 1 tablespoon lemon zest (optional)
- 1 teaspoon black truffle salt

Direction

- Soak six eggs with sous vide insert in a big pot of water; set the heat on 64.5° Celsius or 148.1° Fahrenheit and cook for an hour. Cool the eggs down for 10 minutes in a bowl of lukewarm water.

- On a low stream of water in the faucet, crack the egg carefully with your hands. Allow the white to seep away under the running water. Put the egg yolks in a bowl.
- In another bowl, mix together baking powder, flour, and sea salt. Beat the remaining egg in a separate bowl. Pour breadcrumbs on a dish.
- In a large pot, heat 1 1/2 -in oil to 182°C or 360°F.
- Gently dredge each egg yolk in the flour mix and submerge into the egg wash. Dredge the yolk in the plate with breadcrumbs. Fry the coated yolks in hot oil for half a minute until golden. Place them on a paper towel to drain. Top with truffle salt and lemon zest. Serve.

Nutrition Information

- Calories: 161 calories;
- Total Fat: 8.2
- Sodium: 830
- Total Carbohydrate: 12.5
- Cholesterol: 217

Drenched Fig Boats

Serving: 16

Ingredients

- 3/4 cup soft goat cheese
- 1 tablespoon brandy
- 1 tablespoon honey
- 24 dried figs
- 1/2 cup chopped walnuts

Direction

- Mix honey, brandy and goat cheese in a small bowl.
- Cut fig stems off.
- Use a small spoon/pastry bag to fill with flavored goat cheese.
- Lengthwise, cut each fig in half. To coat, dip cheese side in walnuts.
- Put on serving tray, nuts facing upwards.

Nutrition Information

- Calories: 143 calories;
- Total Fat: 6
- Sodium: 58
- Total Carbohydrate: 20.5
- Cholesterol: 8
- Protein: 3.7

Frozen Grapes

Serving: 4

Ingredients

- 1 cup seedless green grapes
- 1 cup seedless red grapes
- 1/4 cup white sugar

Direction

- Pluck the grapes from its stems then place in a colander. Wash thoroughly.
- Put the grapes in a gallon size ziplock bag.
- Add sugar in the bag then seal; shake it gently to coat the grapes with sugar
- Move grapes on a paper towel; air-dry any remaining water for about 15mins.
- On a baking sheet or shallow pan, place grapes in a single layer then keep in the freezer for at least two hours.

Nutrition Information

- Calories: 105 calories;
- Cholesterol: 0
- Protein: 0.5
- Total Fat: 0.5
- Sodium: 2
- Total Carbohydrate: 26.7

Ahi Poke Basic

Serving: 4

Ingredients

- 1 tablespoon toasted sesame seeds
- 2 pounds fresh tuna steaks, cubed
- 1 cup soy sauce
- 3/4 cup chopped green onions
- 2 tablespoons sesame oil
- 1 tablespoon crushed red pepper (optional)
- 2 tablespoons finely chopped macadamia nuts

Direction

- Mix macadamia nuts, chili pepper, sesame seeds and oil, green onions, soy sauce, and Ahi in a non-reactive medium-sized bowl; blend well. Store in the refrigerator for a minimum of 2 hours prior to serving.

Nutrition Information

- Calories: 396 calories;
- Total Carbohydrate: 8.6
- Cholesterol: 102
- Protein: 58.4
- Total Fat: 13.7
- Sodium: 3696

Apricot Pecan Camembert

Serving: 8

Ingredients

- 1 (8 ounce) round Camembert cheese, cubed
- 1/4 cup apricot preserves
- 1 tablespoon chopped pecans

Direction

- Preheat the oven to 175 degrees C (350 degrees F). Add the Camembert cheese into a shallow oven-proof serving plate.
- Bake in the preheated oven for roughly 20 minutes or till becoming tender. Use pecans and apricot preserves to cover the cheese. Keep baking for roughly 3 minutes longer or till the preserves become thoroughly warm.

Nutrition Information

- Calories: 115 calories;
- Protein: 5.8
- Total Fat: 7.5
- Sodium: 243
- Total Carbohydrate: 6.7
- Cholesterol: 20

Arancini (Italian Rice Balls)

Serving: 24

Ingredients

- 4 ounces mozzarella cheese, diced
- 1/4 cup chopped fresh basil
- 3 teaspoons extra virgin olive oil, divided
- 3 3/4 cups water
- 1 1/3 cups uncooked brown rice
- 2 cloves garlic
- 1 bay leaf
- 1/4 teaspoon salt
- 4 ounces thinly sliced prosciutto, chopped
- 5 egg whites, divided
- 3 tablespoons freshly grated Parmesan cheese
- 1 cup dry bread crumbs
- 3 cups vegetable oil for frying

Direction

In a saucepan, boil water. Mix in rice. Put in salt, garlic and bay leaf. Bring it back to boiling, lower heat to low and simmer, covered, until the rice is tender, about half an hour. Discard from the heat and remove the bay leaf and garlic. Let cool.

Combine basil, mozzarella cheese and prosciutto in a medium bowl. Add 2 teaspoons olive oil over, coat by tossing.

Stir Parmesan cheese and three egg whites into rice until they are well blended. Mix resulting rice mixture into basil and mozzarella mixture until all the ingredients are evenly distributed.

In a deep-fryer, heat 2 inches of oil to 350°F (175°C). Put the breadcrumbs into a shallow bowl. In another shallow bowl, whisk one teaspoon olive oil and 2 remaining of egg whites together.

Wet your hands, form rice mixture into 24 balls. Dip each ball in egg whites, coat with the breadcrumbs. Deep fry rice balls for 30 seconds each batch, a few at a time, until golden brown. Place on the paper towels to drain. Enjoy when it is still hot.

Nutrition Information

- Calories: 122 calories;
- Cholesterol: 8
- Protein: 4.5
- Total Fat: 6.3
- Sodium: 199
- Total Carbohydrate: 11.6

Asian Roll Lettuce Wrap

Serving: 4

Ingredients

- 1 cup brown rice 1/3 cup water
- 3 tablespoons fresh lemon juice
- 2 teaspoons minced garlic
- 1 tablespoon minced fresh ginger root
- 1 teaspoon sugar
- 1 cup water
- 16 large lettuce leaves
- 1 cup shredded carrots
- 1 cup green onions, thinly sliced
- 1 cup sliced red bell pepper
- 1 cup sliced radishes
- 1/3 cup light soy sauce
- 1 pound ground turkey
- 1 tablespoon light soy sauce
- 1 teaspoon minced garlic

- 2 teaspoons minced fresh ginger root

Direction

- Mix 2 tsp. ginger, 1 tsp. minced garlic, 1 tbsp. soy sauce and ground turkey in a medium bowl. Shape to 16 meatballs. Roll to ovals. Cover and refrigerate.
- Mix 2 cups water and rice in a medium saucepan on medium heat. Bring to a boil. Lower heat. Simmer until rice is tender for 20 minutes.
- Preheat broiler or grill. Put into every small bowl or serving platter red peppers, radishes, scallions, carrots, lettuce leaves and rice. Mix sugar, 1 tbsp. ginger, 2 tsp. garlic, lemon juice, 1/3 cup water and 1/3 cup soy sauce in a medium bowl. Divide to 4 small dipping bowls.
- On each 10-inch skewer, thread 2 meatballs. Broil or grill for 10-12 minutes, occasionally turning to brown all sides. Broiling: line aluminum foil on a broiler pan. After 6 minutes, drain fat.

- Eating: On the palm of your hand, put a lettuce leaf. Spoon a bit of rice, meat roll, and a few veggies. Roll up. Dip into dipping sauce or spoon sauce on.

Nutrition Information

- Calories: 369 calories;
- Total Fat: 9.9
- Sodium: 951
- Total Carbohydrate: 42.8
- Cholesterol: 84
- Protein: 28.6

Asparagus Rolantina

Serving: 4

Ingredients

- 4 tablespoons butter, melted
- 1 cup Italian-style dried bread crumbs
- 1 pound fresh green asparagus spears, trimmed
- 4 slices Swiss cheese
- 5 (1/2 ounce) slices prosciutto
- ground black pepper to taste
- 1/2 cup grated Parmesan cheese

Direction

- Preheat an oven to 175 °C or 350 °F.
- Boil a big pot of water. Into the water, put the asparagus, and allow to cook for a minute, for 2 minutes in case spears are thick.
- On a plate, place a slice of meat. Top slice of meat with a cheese slice. At 1 end of cheese and meat Put 3 or 4 asparagus spears, and scatter to taste with black pepper. Roll meat and

cheese up on top of asparagus, and seal using toothpick. In a casserole dish, put the asparagus rolls. When every asparagus roll has been set in casserole dish, put melted butter on the whole dish. Scatter Parmesan cheese and bread crumbs on top.

- Let bake for 15 to 20 minutes, or till crumb mixture has turned to crust on top of asparagus rolls.

Nutrition Information

- Calories: 457 calories;
- Total Fat: 29.5
- Sodium: 1160
- Total Carbohydrate: 27.4
- Cholesterol: 81
- Protein: 21.7

Baba Ghanuj

Serving: 8

Ingredients

- 2 pounds eggplant
- 4 cloves garlic, unpeeled
- 1/4 cup lemon juice
- 2 tablespoons tahini
- 1 1/4 teaspoons salt
- 1 tablespoon olive oil, or to taste
- 1 pinch ground sumac, or to taste

Direction

- Set an oven to preheat to 220°C (425°F). Use fork to pierce the eggplants all over and put it on a baking tray.
- Roast the eggplants in the preheated oven for 10-12 minutes, flipping from time to time, until it becomes tender and charred.
- On a skewer, thread the garlic cloves.
- Roast the garlic in the preheated oven for 6-8 minutes, flipping once, until it becomes tender and charred.
- Allow the garlic and eggplants to cool for about 5 minutes until it becomes easy to touch. Take off the skin and move to a food processor. Add the salt, tahini and lemon juice, then process until it becomes smooth.

- Drizzle olive oil on the eggplant mixture and sprinkle sumac on top.

Nutrition Information

- Calories: 69 calories;
- Cholesterol: 0
- Protein: 1.9
- Total Fat: 3.9
- Sodium: 370
- Total Carbohydrate: 8.5

Bacon Wrapped Dates Stuffed With Blue Cheese

Serving: 32

Ingredients

- 1 pound sliced bacon, cut in half
- 1 pound pitted dates
- 4 ounces blue cheese

Direction

- Set the oven to 190°C or 375°F.
- Halve the dates and open them up. Pinch off blue cheese pieces and put them into the center of the dates. Close the dates halves and use a half-slice of bacon to wrap around the outside. Use a toothpick to secure each one, then arrange on a baking sheet or in a baking dish with sides to catch any grease.
- In the preheated oven, bake about 30-40 minutes, until the bacon is crisp. Turn the dates over after the first 20 minutes for even cooking.

Nutrition Information

- Calories: 78 calories;
- Protein: 2.8
- Total Fat: 3
- Sodium: 157
- Total Carbohydrate: 10.8
- Cholesterol: 8

Baked Goat Cheese Caprese Salad

Serving: 4

Ingredients

- 2 tablespoons olive oil, divided
- 3 tablespoons basil chiffonade (thinly sliced fresh basil leaves), divided
- 1 (4 ounce) log of fresh goat cheese, halved
- 16 cherry tomatoes, cut in half on the diagonal
- freshly ground black pepper to taste
- 1 pinch cayenne pepper, or to taste

Direction

- Set an oven to 200°C (400°F) and start preheating.
- Use around 1 1/2 teaspoons of olive oil to lightly sprinkle into the bottom of each 6-ounce ramekin and use around 1 tablespoon of basil to dust over the oil in each ramekin. In each ramekin, arrange a goat cheese piece over the

basil; with sliced cherry tomatoes put around. Arrange cayenne and cracked black pepper on top. Top each portion with 1 1/2 teaspoons of the remaining basil, arrange ramekins on a baking sheet, and use 1 1/2 teaspoons more of olive oil to lightly sprinkle over each serving.

- Put in the prepared oven and bake for around 15 minutes until bubbling. Serve warm.

Nutrition Information

- Calories: 178 calories;
- Total Fat: 15.5
- Sodium: 152
- Total Carbohydrate: 4.1
- Cholesterol: 22
- Protein: 6.8

Baked Pork Spring Rolls

Serving: 12

Ingredients

- 1/2 pound ground pork
- 1 cup finely shredded cabbage
- 1/4 cup finely shredded carrot
- 2 green onions, thinly sliced
- 2 tablespoons chopped fresh cilantro
- 1/2 teaspoon sesame oil
- 1/2 tablespoon oyster sauce
- 2 teaspoons grated fresh ginger root
- 1 1/2 teaspoons minced garlic
- 1 teaspoon chile sauce
- 1 tablespoon cornstarch
- 1 tablespoon water
- 12 (7 inch square) spring roll wrappers
- 4 teaspoons vegetable oil

Direction

- Preheat the oven to 220 degrees C (425 degrees F).
- Put the pork in a medium saucepan. Then cook over medium-high heat until brown evenly. Take away from heat and let drain.
- Mix carrot, cabbage, pork, chile sauce, sesame oil, oyster sauce, garlic, ginger, cilantro, and green onions in a medium bowl together.
- In a small bowl, blend water and cornstarch.
- Put about a tablespoon of the pork mixture in the center of the spring roll wrappers. Then roll around the mixture, folding the edges inward to stick them together. Make your fingers wet in the mixture of cornstarch and water, then sweep wrapper seams to seal up.
- On a medium baking sheet, place the spring rolls in a single layer. Sweep with vegetable oil. Bake for 20 minutes in the preheated oven, or until hot and lightly browned. To get crispier spring rolls, turn after 10 minutes.

Nutrition Information

- Calories: 154 calories;
- Total Carbohydrate: 20.1
- Cholesterol: 15
- Protein: 6.7

Baked Stuffed Brie With Cranberries Walnuts

Serving: 8

Ingredients

- 1 small wheel of brie (about 6 to 8 inches), chilled
- 1/4 cup dried cranberries
- 1/4 cup chopped walnuts
- 1 sheet frozen puff pastry, thawed, plus extra for (optional) design
- 1 egg, beaten with
- 1 teaspoon water

Direction

- Using a sharp paring knife to score all the way around the side of a wheel of brie. Directly cut on the "equator" through the rind. Wrap a dental floss/a long piece of string on the newly made cut around the brie. Loop one end of the string over the other end (a half knot). Then pull the string's ends in opposite ways, cutting the brie in half.

- On one cut side of the brie, press the dried cranberries; on the other side, press walnut. Put the 2 sides back together quickly with the cranberries over the walnuts. Press together and stuff any walnuts or cranberries that fell out back in.

- On a floured surface, roll a thawed sheet of puff pastry out into an approximately 1/8-inch thick sheet. In center of pastry, lay brie. Pull up edges gently to make sure there is enough dough to wrap the brie entirely. If there is too much dough, trim the corners off. Brush egg wash on dough. Fold one of the dough's edge over the brie, then the other side. Fold the remaining edges over and encase the brie complexly. If necessary, trim excess pieces of dough. Turn the brie in order for the seam to be at the bottom; to snug the dough against the brie, press the sides in gently. Brush egg wash on the sides and top of the wrapped brie.

- If you want to decorate the brie using cut-out shapes of extra puff pastry, use dough that is extremely cold (almost still frozen) to guarantee the sharp lines. Use egg wash to brush decorative pieces lightly. Let the brie sit for an hour in the freezer (this step is crucial; see note below).

- Heat oven to 220°C (425°F) beforehand. Use parchment paper to line a rimmed baking sheet.

- On the prepared baking sheet, lay the brie. In preheated oven, allow to bake on the center rack for approximately 20 minutes till browned and the cheese is leaking. (It is rare if the brie does not leak through, but it takes 20-25 minutes for the cheese to melt and the pastry to get browned.)

Nutrition Information

- Calories: 304 calories;
- Total Fat: 22.3
- Sodium: 261
- Total Carbohydrate: 17.4
- Cholesterol: 49
- Protein: 9.3

Barney's King Salmon Gravlax

Serving: 10

Ingredients

- 1 cup dark brown sugar
- 3/4 cup kosher salt
- 2 tablespoons cracked white peppercorns
- 2 (1 pound) salmon fillets, bones removed
- 1 bunch fresh dill, finely chopped

Direction

- In a bowl, mix peppercorns, salt, and sugar and combine well. Drizzle about 1/3 of mixture on the bottom of a glass baking dish. Put one salmon fillet on top with the skin-side down. Top with a drizzle of 1/2 the dill. Add another 1/3 of sugar mixture to cover. Drizzle the remaining dill onto the second fillet and put skin-side up onto the first fillet. Pour the remaining sugar mixture to cover.
- Use plastic wrap to wrap the baking dish tightly and then chill for 18 hours. Flip the

- fillets over and ladle the syrupy liquid on top of fish before you cover once again using plastic wrap. Chill for another 18 hours.
- Lightly rinse the fillets with cold water to get rid of salt and then pat dry. Thinly chop the fish at an angle.

Nutrition Information

- Calories: 255 calories;
- Protein: 18.3
- Total Fat: 9.9
- Sodium: 6893
- Total Carbohydrate: 22.8
- Cholesterol: 54

Beef Samosas

Serving: 18

Ingredients

- 2 large potatoes, peeled
- 1 cup frozen peas, thawed
- 2 tablespoons vegetable oil
- 1/2 teaspoon cumin seeds
- 1 bay leaf, crushed
- 2 large onions, finely chopped
- 1 pound ground beef
- 4 cloves garlic, crushed
- 1 tablespoon minced fresh ginger root
- 1/2 teaspoon ground black pepper
- 1 1/2 teaspoons salt
- 1 teaspoon ground cumin
- 1 teaspoon ground coriander
- 1 teaspoon ground turmeric
- 1 teaspoon chili powder
- 1/2 teaspoon ground cinnamon
- 1/2 teaspoon ground cardamom

- 2 tablespoons chopped fresh cilantro
- 2 tablespoons chopped green chile peppers
- 1 quart oil for deep frying
- 1 (16 ounce) package phyllo dough

Direction

- In a medium saucepan, boil a slightly salted water. Mix in peas and potatoes. Allow to cook for 15 minutes till potatoes are soft yet remain firm. Let drain, mash together and reserve.
- Over medium-high heat, heat the oil in a big saucepan. Brown bay leaf and cumin seeds. Add in ground beef and onions. Let cook for 5 minutes till onions are tender and beef is equally brown. Add in fresh ginger root and garlic. Put cardamom, cinnamon, chili powder, turmeric, coriander, cumin, salt and black pepper to season. Mix in the mashed potato mixture. Take off from heat and refrigerate for an hour, or till cool.
- In a big, heavy saucepan, heat oil over high heat.
- Into the beef and potato mixture, add green chili peppers and cilantro. Onto every phyllo sheet, put about 1 tablespoon of mixture. Fold the sheets forming triangles, pressing edges together with wet fingers.

- Fry in small batches for 3 minutes till golden brown. Allow to drain on paper towels and serve while warm.

Nutrition Information

Calories: 258 calories;

Cholesterol: 21

Protein: 7.6

Total Fat: 14.8

Sodium: 346

Total Carbohydrate: 23.8

Oyster Motoyaki

Serving: 6

Ingredients

- 6 oysters, scrubbed and shucked
- 1 teaspoon butter
- 1/4 cup chopped fresh mushrooms
- 1/4 cup chopped green onion
- 1 cup Japanese mayonnaise (such as Kewpie®)
- 1 tablespoon red miso paste
- 1 teaspoon ground cayenne pepper
- 1 teaspoon ground black pepper
- 1 tablespoon capelin roe (masago)
- 1 lemon, cut into 6 wedges

Direction

- For preheating, set the oven at 400 degrees Fahrenheit or 200 degrees Celsius.
- Remove oyster meat from their shells and rinse with cold water, removing any shell fragments or pearl beginnings. Pat them dry with paper towels

and cut each into 5 smaller pieces. Rinse the lower half of the shells well, discarding the flat tops.
- In a small skillet, melt butter over a medium heat and add green onion along with the mushrooms. Cook and stir for 5 minutes until softened.
- In a small bowl, whisk together black pepper, cayenne, red miso, and mayonnaise. Spread the mixture into a thin layer on the bottom of each shells.
- Divide the oyster meat among the shells and top with mushroom mixture. Thickly cover with the remaining mayonnaise mixture and arrange the shells on a baking sheet.
- Bake in preheated oven on the top rack for 20-25 minutes until the tops turn dark brown.
- Garnish with roe and serve the baked oysters with lemon wedges.

Nutrition Information

- Calories: 348 calories;
- Total Fat: 32
- Sodium: 423

- Total Carbohydrate: 8.4
- Cholesterol: 63
- Protein: 9

Blue Cheese And Pear Tartlets

Serving: 15

Ingredients

- 4 ounces blue cheese, crumbled
- 1 ripe pear - peeled, cored, and chopped
- 2 tablespoons light cream
- ground black pepper to taste
- 1 (2.1 ounce) package mini phyllo tart shells

Direction

- Prepare the phyllo shells following the package instructions; set aside and cool.
- Combine cream, pear, and blue cheese; sprinkle pepper to taste. Scoop the mixture into the cooled phyllo shells.
- Bake in a 175°C or 350°F oven for 15 minutes. Serve hot.

Nutrition Information

- Calories: 60 calories;
- Total Fat: 3.6
- Sodium: 116
- Total Carbohydrate: 4.5
- Cholesterol: 7
- Protein: 2.2

Boranie Bademjan (Persian Eggplant Yogurt Dip)

Serving: 4

Ingredients

- 2 (1 pound) eggplants
- 2/3 cup Greek yogurt
- 4 cloves garlic, peeled and crushed
- 4 teaspoons chopped fresh mint
- 2 teaspoons fresh lime juice
- 1 teaspoon olive oil
- 1 teaspoon salt
- 1/2 teaspoon freshly ground black pepper
- 1/4 teaspoon powdered saffron (optional)
- 2 teaspoons hot water (optional)
- 1 sprig fresh mint, stemmed
- 1 teaspoon Greek yogurt

Direction

- Heat an oven to 175°C or 350°F. Line aluminum foil on a baking sheet.
- Puncture eggplants entirely using fork; arrange on baking sheet.
- Bake for 40 minutes in prepped oven, flipping often, till tender.
- Transfer the eggplants onto a chopping board and rest for 8 - 10 minutes, till cool enough to work with. Remove the skin; chop the flesh.
- In a bowl, mix pepper, salt, olive oil, lime juice, 4 teaspoons of chopped mint, garlic, 2/3 cup of Greek yogurt and eggplant flesh; stir well. Scoop to serving dish.
- In small-size bowl, dissolve saffron in hot water; sprinkle on mixture of eggplant. Jazz up using a teaspoon of Greek yogurt and mint leaves.

Brie And Mushroom Phyllo Puffs

Serving: 25

Ingredients

- 1 cup butter, divided
- 8 crimini mushrooms, sliced
- 6 shiitake mushrooms, sliced
- 3 cloves garlic, chopped
- 1 (8 ounce) wedge Brie cheese
- 1 (16 ounce) package frozen phyllo pastry, thawed

Direction

- Place a skillet over medium heat and melt 2 1/2 tablespoons of butter. Sauté garlic, shiitake mushrooms, and crimini until tender. Remove from the heat, set aside. Microwave the leftover butter in a dish until melted.
- Preheat oven to 190°C/375°F.

- Roll out phyllo dough and cut equally into three 3 x 12-inch strips using kitchen shears. Place two phyllo sheets on either a cutting board or another work surface. Use a damp paper towel to cover the pile of remaining sheets to prevent them from drying.
- Brush melted butter on the top sheet. Put a dab of brie (around the size of a raspberry) on one end of the sheet. Then add a small amount of mushroom mixture on top of brie. Make a triangle by folding the dough over the filling. Continue to fold back and forth in a triangle shape and brush the exposed side with melted butter as you go. Seal the last fold with a little butter or water. Place the phyllo triangle on an ungreased baking sheet. Repeat process with the rest of the dough and filling.
- Bake in preheated oven for 20 to 25 minutes, or until triangles are golden brown. Turnover once while baking to brown the other side.

Nutrition Information

- Calories: 153 calories;
- Protein: 3.6
- Total Fat: 11
- Sodium: 199
- Total Carbohydrate: 10
- Cholesterol: 29

Broiled Mochi With Nori Seaweed

Serving: 8

Ingredients

- 8 frozen mochi squares
- 1/2 cup soy sauce
- 1 sheet nori (dry seaweed)

Direction

- Preheat an oven to 275 degrees C (450 degrees F).
- Dunk the mochi into the soy sauce and put in a baking sheet. Bake for around five minutes or until heated through.
- As the mochi cooks, slice dried seaweed into eight strips. Put these strips into a large frying pan on medium heat. Remove them from heat when warmed after about 1 to 2 minutes.
- Encase every mochi cake with seaweed and then serve warm.

Nutrition Information

- Calories: 109 calories;
- Cholesterol: 0
- Protein: 3.1
- Total Fat: 0.2
- Sodium: 907
- Total Carbohydrate: 23.1

Bruschetta With Roasted Sweet Red Peppers

Serving: 12

Ingredients

- 16 ounces Italian bread
- 2 tablespoons olive oil
- 1 (16 ounce) jar marinated roasted sweet red peppers
- 3 cloves garlic, chopped
- 1 tomato, seeded and chopped
- 1 cup chopped fresh basil
- 1 onion, chopped (optional)
- 3 teaspoons balsamic vinegar

Direction

- Preheat broiler.
- Cut 1-inch thick slices of bread. Brush olive oil over one side of each slice of bread. Broil until toast is slightly golden, oil-side up. Transfer off the broiler pan and allow the toast to cool.

- Mix onion, basil, tomatoes, garlic, and roasted pepper in a medium-sized bowl. Evenly sprinkle the mixture over each toast. Drizzle on some balsamic vinegar, then serve.

Nutrition Information

- Calories: 143 calories;
- Total Carbohydrate: 22.7
- Cholesterol: 0
- Protein: 4.2
- Total Fat: 3.8
- Sodium: 358

Buckwheat Grissini With Real Butter (Gluten Free)

Serving: 2

Ingredients

- 1/3 cup buckwheat flour
- 1/3 cup finely grated Parmigiano-Reggiano cheese
- 1/4 cup gluten-free all-purpose flour
- 2 tablespoons butter, divided
- 1 tablespoon black sesame seeds
- 1 tablespoon fresh thyme leaves
- 3 tablespoons water, or more as needed

Direction

- Preheat the oven to 175°C or 350°F. Line parchment paper on a baking sheet.
- Combine in bowl with 1 1/2 tablespoons of butter, gluten-free flour, Parmigiano-Reggiano cheese and buckwheat flour using your hands till mixture looks much like small pebbles. Stir

in thyme and sesame seeds. Put in water, a tablespoon at one time, till mixture holds together to soft dough.

- Split dough to make 6 pieces. Rest dough for five minutes.
- Form every piece of dough into a lengthy, thinnish rope approximately 6- to 7-inch long. Place on baking sheet, next to each. Brush dough with leftover 1 1/2 teaspoon of butter.
- Bake for 20 minutes in prepped oven till browned fully. Cool through for 10 minutes prior to serving.

Nutrition Information

- Calories: 309 calories;
- Total Carbohydrate: 28.5
- Cholesterol: 42
- Protein: 10.3
- Total Fat: 18.8
- Sodium: 289

Buddhist Monk Dumplings

Serving: 10

Ingredients

- 1 potato
- 2 teaspoons vegetable oil
- 1 tablespoon mustard seed
- 1/4 teaspoon cumin seeds
- 2 carrots, finely diced
- 1 onion, finely chopped
- 1 green chile, finely chopped
- 1 clove garlic, finely chopped
- 1 teaspoon ground turmeric
- 1 teaspoon grated ginger
- 1/2 cup finely shredded cabbage
- 1/4 (14 ounce) package firm tofu, crumbled
- 1/2 cup water
- 1/4 cup chopped fresh cilantro
- 1 teaspoon garam masala
- salt to taste

- Pastry:
- 3 cups all-purpose flour
- 1 cup water
- 1 pinch salt

Direction

- In a large pot filled with salted water, add the potatoes and bring to a boil. Reduce to medium-low heat; simmer for 20 minutes, or until potatoes are tender. Drain and mash the potatoes, then set aside to cool.
- Place a skillet over medium heat and heat the oil. Add cumin seeds and mustard seeds; stir. Add ginger, turmeric, garlic, green chile, onion, and carrots and cook while stirring for 1 minute. Add tofu, cabbage, and the mashed potatoes; stir. Add cilantro and water and cook for 7 to 8 minutes, or until water dries up and vegetables are tender. Stir in salt and garam masala well. Remove from the heat and allow to cool.
- In a bowl, mix together salt, water, and flour. Knead into a ball and continue to knead for 10 to 12 minutes, or until dough is soft. Wrap and let dough rest for at least 1 hour.
- Roll out a knob of dough into a small round with a diameter of 4 inches. Add a full teaspoon of filling in the center, moisten edges with a bit of water. Press the edges together, allowing to

overlap the top slightly to form a pleat. Form half-moon shapes with the pleats around the edges. Repeat process with the rest of the filling and dough.

- Fit a steamer basket in a large pan. Add water reaching 2 inches deep and bring to a boil. Steam the dumplings for 15 minutes, or until cooked through and swollen.

Nutrition Information

- Calories: 188 calories;
- Total Carbohydrate: 36.2
- Cholesterol: 0
- Total Fat: 2.2
- Protein: 5.8
- Sodium: 46

Burrata Bruschetta With Figs

Serving: 4

Ingredients

- 12 Black Mission figs, halved lengthwise
- 2 tablespoons balsamic vinegar
- 2 tablespoons extra virgin olive oil
- 6 ounces Burrata cheese, thickly sliced
- 6 (1/2 inch thick) slices Italian bread, toasted
- sea salt and ground black pepper to taste

Direction

- Preheat outdoor grill to high heat. Oil the grate lightly.
- On grill, put figs, skin-side down. Cook for 2-4 minutes until they start to bubble and swell.
- Whisk olive oil and balsamic vinegar for 1 minute until combined completely.
- On each toast piece, top it with Burrata cheese. Spread figs around the bread. Drizzle balsamic

vinegar mixture on it. Season to taste with black pepper and sea salt.

Nutrition Information

- Calories: 377 calories;
- Total Fat: 17.3
- Sodium: 364
- Total Carbohydrate: 44.9
- Cholesterol: 30
- Protein: 9.8

Cantonese Style Pork And Shrimp Dumplings

Serving: 10

Ingredients

- 1/4 pound ground pork
- 1 cup chopped watercress
- 1/2 (8 ounce) can water chestnuts, drained and chopped
- 1/4 cup chopped green onions
- 1 tablespoon oyster sauce
- 1 1/2 tablespoons sesame oil
- 1 teaspoon minced garlic
- 1 teaspoon soy sauce
- 1/8 teaspoon ground white pepper
- 1/8 teaspoon salt
- 1 (16 ounce) package round dumpling skins
- 1 pound peeled and deveined medium shrimp

Direction

- Mix thoroughly pork, oyster sauce, soy sauce, watercress, garlic, green onion, salt, ground white pepper, water chestnuts, and sesame oil in a large bowl.
- Spoon a half teaspoonful of filling into each dumpling skin. Add one shrimp into the filling. Wet the edge of the dumpling skin slightly and then fold it over. Pinch the skin with your finger to seal the fillings all over.
- To cook: Heat oil in a large skillet over medium heat and cook the dumplings for 15 minutes, flipping it over halfway through. You can also cook the dumplings by placing them in a pot with boiling water for 10 minutes. Let them drain and serve them together with hot chicken broth.

Nutrition Information

- Calories: 234 calories;
- Protein: 15.8
- Total Fat: 5.9
- Sodium: 402
- Total Carbohydrate: 28.2
- Cholesterol: 81

Caponata Sauce

Serving: 12

Ingredients

- 1 pound eggplant, peeled and cut into 1/2-inch cubes
- salt as needed
- extra-virgin olive oil, or as needed
- 1 cup chopped onion
- 1 cup chopped celery
- 1 green bell pepper, cut into 1/4-inch cubes
- 1 1/2 cups canned Italian plum tomatoes, chopped
- 1 1/2 teaspoons chopped anchovies
- 1 pinch dried basil
- 1 pinch dried oregano
- 1/4 cup chopped green olives
- 1 tablespoon drained capers
- 1 tablespoon red wine vinegar, or more to taste
- freshly ground black pepper
- 1/2 cup toasted pine nuts
- 4 leaves lettuce (optional)

- 1 cup 1/2-inch thick French bread toasts (optional)
- 4 tomato wedges (optional)

Direction

- Set the eggplant in a colander. Sprinkle the eggplant with a generous amount of salt. Allow the eggplant to sit for 30 minutes until drained. Squeeze the eggplant to release excess water.
- Put olive oil in a large skillet and heat it over medium heat. Cook the eggplant for 5-10 minutes until golden brown. Place the eggplant into a bowl. Leave the remaining oil into the skillet.
- Cook the green bell pepper, celery, and onion in the same skillet for 5-10 minutes, stirring and adding more oil if necessary until softened. Mix basil, oregano, tomatoes, anchovies, and eggplant into the onion mixture. Cook the mixture for 2-3 minutes over high heat until thickened. Remove the skillet from the heat. Allow the mixture to cool for at least 15 minutes to room temperature.
- Stir the capers and olives into the eggplant mixture. Drizzle mixture with more olive oil and red wine vinegar. Season the mixture with salt and pepper. Add the pine nuts.
- Use lettuce leaves to line the plate. Spread the toasts with the eggplant mixture. Arrange the

toasts onto the lettuce and garnish them with tomato wedges.

Nutrition Information

- Calories: 94 calories;
- Total Carbohydrate: 8.7
- Cholesterol: 1
- Protein: 2.9
- Total Fat: 5.9
- Sodium: 198

Chef John's Asparagus Tart

Serving: 1

Ingredients

- 1 6x9-inch sheet frozen puff pastry, thawed
- 6 spears fresh asparagus, trimmed
- 1 tablespoon Dijon mustard
- 1 1/2 teaspoons creme fraiche
- 1 pinch ground black pepper
- 1 pinch cayenne pepper
- 2 teaspoons butter, melted
- 2 tablespoons freshly grated Parmigiano-Reggiano cheese, or to taste

Direction

- Preheat the oven to 200 °C or 400 °F. Line a silicone baking mat on a baking sheet.
- On the prepped baking sheet, lay out puff pastry. To form a half-inch wide border, fold edges up. Puncture inner base of dough fully using a fork.

- In the prepped oven, bake for 10 minutes till puffed and golden. To deflate, push puffed middle down using back of a fork.

- Boil a big pot of slightly salted water. Put asparagus and allow to cook without cover for a minute till bright green. Let drain in colander and quickly dunk in ice water for few minutes till cold to end the cooking process. Allow to drain.

- In a small bowl, mix cayenne pepper, black pepper, creme fraiche and mustard together; scatter into the base of cooled tart shell. Put the asparagus spears, clipping as needed to suit the tart shell, in the middle of tart over the mustard spread. Glaze top of asparagus and crust with melted butter and over the top, scatter Parmigiano-Reggiano cheese.

- In the oven, bake for 10 to 12 minutes till asparagus is soft and pastry is browned.

Nutrition Information

- Calories: 795 calories;
- Sodium: 869
- Total Carbohydrate: 58.8
- Cholesterol: 40
- Protein: 14.6

Pate De Campagne

Serving: 12

Ingredients

- Pate Spice:
- 1 teaspoon ground cloves
- 1 teaspoon ground nutmeg
- 1 teaspoon ground ginger
- 1 teaspoon cayenne pepper
- Pate:
- 1 1/4 pounds boneless pork shoulder, cut into 1-inch cubes
- 6 ounces duck leg meat
- 4 ounces fatty bacon, chopped
- 4 ounces chicken livers, roughly chopped
- 1 small yellow onion, diced
- 1 shallot, thinly sliced
- 1/3 cup chopped Italian parsley
- 1/4 cup cognac
- 5 teaspoons kosher salt
- 4 cloves garlic, minced

- 1 teaspoon freshly ground black pepper
- 1/8 teaspoon pink curing salt (such as Instacure™ #1) (optional)
- 1/2 cup heavy whipping cream
- 1/3 cup dry bread crumbs
- 2 eggs
- 1/2 cup dried cherries (optional)
- 1/2 cup shelled whole pistachios (optional)
- 8 strips bacon, or as needed

Direction

- To make a spice mixture, put cayenne pepper, ginger, nutmeg and cloves together in a small size bowl then mix.
- Get a large size bowl then combine together the pink curing salt, 3/4 teaspoon spice mixture, pepper, garlic, salt, cognac, parsley, shallot, onion, chicken livers, chopped bacon, duck meat and pork shoulder. Mix well until well combined. Use a plastic wrap to cover and place inside the refrigerator for 2 hours.
- Beat eggs, bread crumbs and cream together in a bowl.
- Put a silicone mat or parchment in a rimmed baking sheet to line then place the pork mixture in it. Let it chill for 15 to 20 minutes to smoothed and grind the meat easier.

- Use a meat-grinder which is attach to a stand mixer to grind the pork mixture into a bowl. Stir in pistachios and dried cherries. Then the cream mixture; slowly fold until mixed well.
- Organize the bacon strips in a crosswise into a 9x15-inch loaf pan, allowing the ends to hang on every edges of the pan. To fit the ends of the pan, cut some strips. Put ground pork mixture on top to fill the pan; flattened the top to smooth. Use a piece of parchment cut that fits the top of the pan to cover; then use a heavy duty aluminum foil to wrap tightly.
- Prepare the oven by preheating to 350 degrees F (175 degrees C).
- Get a deep pot or Dutch oven to place the pan in it. Add in warm top water to reach 1/2 to 1/3 of the way up to the side of the pan. Then cover.
- Place inside the preheated oven for 1 3/4 to 2 hours until an instant-read thermometer used reads 155 degrees F (68 degrees C).
- Then put the pan to a paper-towel lined surface to suck up the moisture. When the mixture begins to rise and reached top edge of the pan, push down using a heavy pan. Discard the aluminum foil, with parchment paper left on top. Get a baking dish lined with paper-towel and put the pan in it. Use aluminum foil to wrap and put on the parchment paper. Push down using some weights like canned food.

- Place inside the refrigerator for 8 hours and let it chill then flatten the pate.
- Put a very warm water into a large bowl to unmold the pate. Then sink the mold for 1 to 2 seconds into warm water. Then place onto paper-towel lined dish; and let it chill again to be ready for slicing and serve.

Nutrition Information

- Calories: 249 calories;
- Total Fat: 14.7
- Sodium: 1121
- Total Carbohydrate: 10.6
- Cholesterol: 114
- Protein: 15

Chevre With Urfa And Crushed Nibs

Serving: 10

Ingredients

- 1 (8 ounce) log of fresh goat cheese (chevre)
- 1/2 teaspoon Urfa biber, or to taste
- 2 tablespoons finely crushed cocoa nibs

Direction

- Put the goat cheese into a bowl, leave aside to room temperature for about 30 minutes. Stir in the Urfa biber until combined well. Spoon the goat cheese onto a work surface lined with a piece of plastic wrap. Wrap plastic over the cheese to create a log shape. Twist both ends of the plastic, refrigerate the goat cheese log in no less than 1 hour.
- Put cocoa nibs on a big and flat plate, unwrap the goat cheese log onto the nibs, toss to cover the surface. Use plastic wrap to refold the cheese back

to the log shape, refrigerate until firm, about an hour more.
- Preserve. Set to room temperature before serving.

Nutrition Information

- Calories: 96 calories;
- Cholesterol: 18
- Protein: 5
- Total Fat: 7.6
- Sodium: 119
- Total Carbohydrate: 1.7

Chicken Liver Pate

Serving: 8

Ingredients

- 1 tablespoon butter
- 1 clove garlic, peeled and chopped
- 1 tablespoon chopped onion
- 1/4 pound chicken livers, trimmed and chopped
- 2 tablespoons dry sherry
- 1/3 (8 ounce) package cream cheese, softened
- hot sauce to taste
- salt and pepper to taste

Direction

- Place a medium size saucepan on the stove and turn on to medium heat then put the butter to melt.
- Add in the onion, garlic, and chicken livers then stir.
- Lower the heat, and gently cook for about 10 minutes until the pink color in chicken faded.

- Transfer the chicken liver mixture in a blender with salt, pepper, hot sauce, cream cheese and dry sherry.
- Blend well until smooth. Place into a medium bowl the mixture then cover and put inside the refrigerator for 2 hours to chill then serve.

Nutrition Information

- Calories: 66 calories;
- Cholesterol: 63
- Protein: 3.2
- Total Fat: 5.4
- Sodium: 70
- Total Carbohydrate: 1.1

Chicken, Artichoke, And Spinach Stuffed Portobellos

Serving: 4

Ingredients

- 1 1/2 pounds skinless, boneless chicken breasts, chopped
- 1 (15 ounce) jar Alfredo sauce
- 1 (10 ounce) package frozen chopped spinach, thawed and squeezed dry
- 1 (7.5 ounce) jar quartered artichoke hearts, drained and chopped
- 1 teaspoon red pepper flakes
- 1 (6 ounce) package shredded Parmesan cheese, divided
- 4 large portobello mushroom caps, stems and gills removed
- 1 tablespoon olive oil

- salt and ground black pepper to taste

Direction

- In a large bowl, add 4 ounces of Parmesan cheese, red pepper flakes, artichoke hearts, spinach, Alfredo sauce and chicken and stir well.
- Using your hands, gently rub the outside of each portobello with olive oil; add salt and pepper for seasoning.
- Distribute the chicken filling evenly among the mushroom caps, then sprinkle with remaining Parmesan cheese. Arrange the mushroom caps on the grill pan of Panasonic Countertop Induction Oven.
- Press "Auto Cook". Choose Poultry with Vegetables setting then press "Start". Turn the dial to choose 2 pounds and press "Start" again. Cook for about 23 minutes until mushrooms are tender and chicken is no longer pink.

Nutrition Information

- Calories: 762 calories;
- Cholesterol: 177
- Protein: 61.4
- Total Fat: 51.1
- Sodium: 2180
- Total Carbohydrate: 16

Chinese Tea Leaf Eggs

Serving: 8

Ingredients

- 8 eggs
- 1 teaspoon salt
- 3 cups water
- 1 tablespoon soy sauce
- 1 tablespoon black soy sauce
- 1/4 teaspoon salt
- 2 tablespoons black tea leaves
- 2 pods star anise
- 1 (2 inch) piece cinnamon stick
- 1 tablespoon tangerine zest

Direction

- Mix a teaspoon of salt and eggs in a big saucepan then pour in cold water to cover; boil.
- Lower heat and let it simmer 20 minutes; take off heat. Drain eggs and let them cool down.

- Once cool enough to handle, crack the shells of the egg by tapping it with the back of a spoon. Do not detach the shells.
- Mix together tangerine zest, three cups water, cinnamon stick, soy sauce, star anise, black soy sauce, tea leaves, and salt in a big saucepan; boil.
- Lower heat and let it simmer, covered, 3 hours; take off heat. Put in eggs and let it steep for a minimum of 8 hours.

Nutrition Information

- Calories: 76 calories;
- Sodium: 659
- Total Carbohydrate: 1.2
- Cholesterol: 186
- Protein: 6.6
- Total Fat: 5

Chocolate Sea Salt Crostini

Serving: 12

Ingredients

- 1 French baguette, cut into diagonal 1/2 inch slices
- extra virgin olive oil
- 4 ounces high-quality dark chocolate, broken into 1-inch pieces
- 1 tablespoon flaked sea salt

Direction

- Turn on the oven's broiler and start preheating. Place the oven rack about 6 inches from the heat source. Line parchment paper or a silicon baking mat on a baking sheet.
- Place baguette slices on the baking sheet in a single layer. Put under broiler and broil for 2 minutes until turning golden. Flip each slice over and broil for an additional 2 minutes. Turn off broiler.
- Flip each of bread slices over again; sprinkle olive oil on top of each slice. Push a chocolate piece into the center of each slice and return to

oven for another 2 minutes. Remove from oven and lightly sprinkle sea salt on top of each chocolate piece.

Nutrition Information

- Calories: 176 calories;
- Total Fat: 8.3
- Sodium: 625
- Total Carbohydrate: 21.3
- Cholesterol: 1
- Protein: 4

Chourico Breakfast Salsa

Serving: 4

Ingredients

- 1 small onion, chopped
- 1/4 pound Portuguese hot chourico sausage
- 1 large tomato, coarsely chopped
- 3 drops hot sauce
- 1 small chile pepper, diced (optional)
- 1/2 teaspoon fresh lime juice (optional)

Direction

- Apply cooking spray to a moderate-sized nonstick skillet, then heat on moderate and stir in onion. Cook and stir for 5 minutes, until onion is tender and translucent.
- Cut the sausage thinly then chop into 1/4" cubes. Stir into the skillet with onions.
- Stir into the sausage mixture with tomato and turn heat to moderately high. If wanted, stir in chile pepper. Blend in the hot sauce, then cook whole mixture for 10-15 minutes while stirring

- sometimes, until liquid has evaporated almost and tomato is broken down.
- Take away from heat and stir in lime juice, then serve warm.

Nutrition Information

- Calories: 112 calories;
- Sodium: 257
- Total Carbohydrate: 5
- Cholesterol: 20
- Protein: 4.8
- Total Fat: 8.3

Cold Roasted Moroccan Spiced Salmon

Serving: 6

Ingredients

- 3/4 teaspoon ground cinnamon
- 3/4 teaspoon ground cumin
- 1/2 teaspoon salt
- 1/2 teaspoon ground ginger
- 1/4 teaspoon mustard powder
- 1/4 teaspoon ground nutmeg
- 1/8 teaspoon cayenne pepper
- 1/8 teaspoon ground allspice
- 2 teaspoons white sugar
- 2 pounds (1-inch thick) boneless, skin-on center-cut salmon fillets
- 1 tablespoon fresh lime juice

Direction

- Mix the cinnamon, salt, cumin, ginger, nutmeg, mustard, cayenne, sugar, and allspice in a small bowl. Let it rest.
- Use a foil to line a baking sheet, then use nonstick cooking spray to coat it. Use cold water to rinse the salmon, then dry with paper towels. Sprinkle the skin lightly with some spice mix, and place the salmon on the baking sheet with its skin downward. Use the leftover spice mix to rub evenly on the salmon.
- Leave the salmon to warm to room temperature for 30 to 40 minutes.
- Prepare an oven by heating it to 220 degrees C or 425 degrees F.
- Drizzle it with some lime juice and leave in the oven for 12 minutes to roast. Remove the salmon from the oven. Let it stand for 15 minutes at room temperature. It should still be rare when taken out of the oven, but it will continue to cook as it stands. Then, after 15 minutes, use foil to wrap the fish tightly and place in the fridge for a minimum of two hours until it's time to serve.

Nutrition Information

- Calories: 225 calories;
- Sodium: 261
- Total Carbohydrate: 2.2
- Cholesterol: 84
- Protein: 30.2
- Total Fat: 9.8

Crab Stuffed Mushrooms

Serving: 10

Ingredients

- 20 large fresh mushrooms, stems removed
- 3 tablespoons Italian-style salad dressing
- 1 cup crabmeat
- 3/4 cup bread crumbs
- 2 eggs, beaten
- 1/4 cup mayonnaise
- 1/4 cup minced onion
- 1 teaspoon lemon juice

Direction

- Set the oven to 375°F (190°C), and start preheating. Grease a cookie sheet with a non-stick cooking spray.
- In a shallow bowl, place mushrooms into Italian dressing to marinate for 20 minutes. Drain completely.
- In a small mixing bowl, mix together lemon juice, onions, mayonnaise, eggs, 1/2 cup of

breadcrumbs and crabmeat. Stuff the mushroom caps with the mixture. Place the mushrooms on the baking sheet. Sprinkle with remaining breadcrumbs.

- Bake in the oven for 15 minutes.

Nutrition Information

- Calories: 124 calories;
- Total Fat: 7.4
- Sodium: 225
- Total Carbohydrate: 8.5
- Cholesterol: 51
- Protein: 6.6

Crab And Lobster Stuffed Mushrooms

Serving: 8

Ingredients

- 3/4 cup melted butter, divided
- 1 pound fresh mushrooms, stems removed
- 1 cup crushed seasoned croutons
- 1 cup shredded mozzarella cheese
- 1 (6 ounce) can crabmeat, drained
- 1 pound lobster tail, cleaned and chopped
- 3 tablespoons minced garlic
- 1/4 cup shredded mozzarella cheese (optional)

Direction

- Preheat an oven to 190 degrees C (375 degrees F). Use about 1/4 cup of melted butter to rub a large baking sheet. Spread a single layer of mushroom caps on the baking sheet.
- Combine crushed croutons, garlic, remaining 1/2 cup of butter, lobster, crabmeat, and shredded cheese in a medium bowl. Place a

spoonful of mixture into mushroom caps where stems were in place.
- Bake in the preheated oven for about 10 to 12 minutes or until browned lightly on top. If desired, drizzle with more cheese and then serve while still hot!

Nutrition Information

- Calories: 310 calories;
- Sodium: 535
- Total Carbohydrate: 6.9
- Cholesterol: 130
- Protein: 21.9
- Total Fat: 22

Creamy Garlic Escargot

Serving: 4

Ingredients

- 4 sheets phyllo dough
- 4 teaspoons butter, melted
- 32 helix snails, without shells
- 2 cups heavy whipping cream
- 4 egg yolks
- 4 tablespoons butter
- 2 tablespoons minced garlic
- 1/4 cup dry white wine
- salt and pepper to taste

Direction

- Preheat oven to 175°C/350°F. Lightly spray non-stick cooking spray over a cupcake pan.
- On a flat surface, place the phyllo dough and brush melted butter over each sheet. Place sheets in layers over the each other. Cut the layered dough into fours. Press each portion of

dough into the cupcake pan and form cups with the dough.

- Bake the cups until golden, about 10 to 15 minutes.
- Drain snails, rinse under running water until liquid is clear. Mix together egg yolks and heavy cream in a small bowl.
- In a sauté pan, melt butter. Then add garlic; cook until garlic is aromatic. Add white wine and snails and sauté for several minutes. Add the heavy cream mixture to the pan and bring to a boil. Add salt and pepper to season. While cooling, the sauce will thicken.
- Remove phyllo cups from the cupcake pan. Plate a phyllo cup on either a bowl or plate. Fill cups with 8 snails each; let cups overflow. Around the cups, pour the cream sauce.

Nutrition Information

- Calories: 786 calories;
- Protein: 25.9
- Total Fat: 65.5
- Sodium: 397
- Total Carbohydrate: 21.9
- Cholesterol: 461

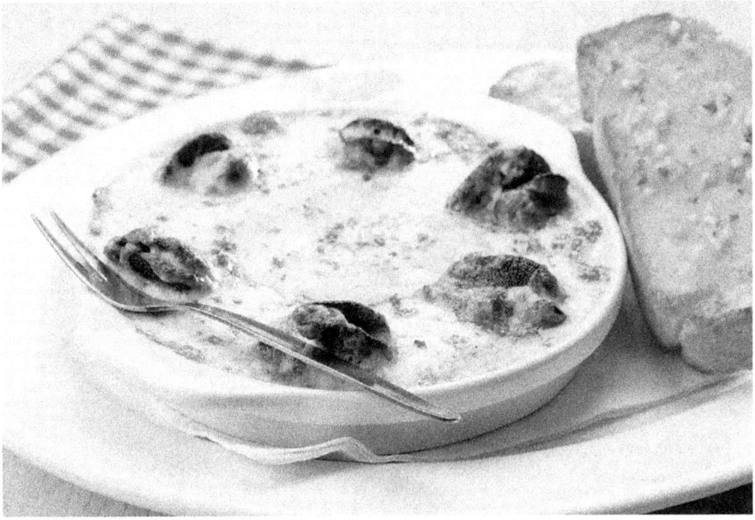

THANK YOU

Thank you for choosing *Quick & Easy Cooking for Beginners* for improving your cooking skills! I hope you enjoyed making the recipes as much as tasting them! If you're interested in learning new recipes and new meals to cook, go and check out the other books of the series.

CPSIA information can be obtained
at www.ICGtesting.com
Printed in the USA
BVHW040504120521
607043BV00004B/1026

9 781802 674750